Cobblestones cottages & castles III

David Young

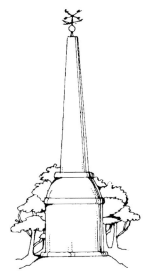

OBELISK PUBLICATIONS

ALSO BY THE AUTHOR:
Cobblestones, Cottages & Castles
More … Cobblestones, Cottages & Castles
An A to Z of Villages
Where's the Dog?

*T*his book is dedicated to
the Ladies and Gentlemen of the Press

All properties are open to the public unless indicated otherwise

Published in association with Westcountry Television and Young Productions
Based on the Television Series "Cobblestones, Cottages and Castles" produced for Westcountry Television by Young Productions

First published in 1994 by
Obelisk Publications
2 Church Hill, Pinhoe, Exeter, Devon EX4 9ER, England
Design and Layout by Chips and Sally Barber
Printed in Great Britain by
Maslands Limited, Tiverton, Devon

© David Young 1994
ISBN: 1 899073 05 1

CONTENTS

Acknowledgements

My thanks to:

The National Trust

Dartmoor National Park Authority

Westcountry Television Ltd

John Prescott Thomas and Jane Clarke for providing me with the opportunity to make this series of *Cobblestones, Cottages and Castles.*

Edward Woodward OBE, a fellow traveller of the West Country, for his kind Foreword

Publishers John Murray for permission to quote from *Church Poems* by John Betjeman, first published in 1981.

The crew: Jeff Booth, Director;

Roger Edwards, Camera; Ray Buxton, Sound; Penni Western, PA; Ray Memmott, Pat Morris, Paul Brown, Editors; Phill Downing, Lights; Norman Earnshaw, Dubbing; Ian Harrold, Graphics.

Geoffrey Bullivant and Margot Young, my co-directors of Young Productions (South West) Ltd

Margot Young for the many hours she worked to produce the typescript

Lord Courtenay

Simon Wingfield Digby

Graham Ovenden

John Rous

Trago Mills Ltd

Cedric Charles Dickens

William Parish

Betty Parr

Lance and June Stapely

The Sidmouth Arts Club Operatic Society

Roy Pickering and the TUC Library

Jennifer Bate, a charming and talented organist

"Oliver"

Sally and Chips Barber, thoughtful and considerate publishers

And to all those lovely people who so kindly allowed me and the film crew into their homes, pubs and churches.

Plate Acknowledgements

All sketches, plans and majority of photographs by the author.

Thanks to Chips Barber for photographs on pages:

9, 10, 12, 13, 15, 18-22, 38, 39, 47 (top left), 56, 57 (top and bottom left), 68, 72, 73, 82, 83, 84, 91.

Edward and Michelle Woodward for page 7

Mid Devon Advertiser for page 37

John B. Gurd (Bridport News) for page 48

Alan Abbott for pages 67 and 69

C. Pelosi, World in Miniature, for page 85

Evening Herald, Plymouth for page 88

Lance Stapley for page 89

Front Cover of Model Village, Babbacombe and cottage at Branscombe by Chips Barber

Back Cover at Warleggan Church by the author

Foreword

by Edward Woodward, OBE

I t has been said that "The soul of 'a people' is its history, historians therefore are the keepers of that soul". If ever there was a 'keeper' of the West Country soul it is David Young – a presenter of great distinction, a producer, writer and historian.

In all his books and programmes David joyously takes us through the lanes and byways – along ancient tracks to half-forgotten villages untouched, it seems, by time.

He leads us to people who and places that enrich this glorious West Country. You can see that this part of the world features greatly in the life of David Young, together with his lovely, and equally enthusiastic, wife Margot, and William and Oliver, his dogs past and present. Devon, Dorset, Somerset and Cornwall fill his life with passionate care.

This is the third of the "Cobblestones" series in which he passes on to us his love of the region. I hope you will read and enjoy and I hope you will come and explore every part of David Young's Glorious West Country.

Edward Woodward OBE

CORNWALL - June 1994

∽ *One* ∽
COTTAGES

T o most of us the English country cottage, with its thatched roof, colour-washed walls and roses round the door, epitomises our heart's desire, the perfect home in idyllic surroundings.

But it wasn't always so. Many thatched cottages, with their cob walls, so highly sought after today, often as second homes, were once hovels. In them one or more families existed, you can hardly say lived, well below the poverty line, in slum conditions.

Cottages at Broadhembury

Gittisham

The majority of ordinary English folk lived in such places, moving into towns and cities during the Industrial Revolution, tempted by a wage, which took them just above starvation level. It was a new sort of home altogether, densely packed terraces of houses, with little in the way of sanitary arrangements. At the end of the day they were merely swapping one form of poverty for another.

I don't want to put you off your dream cottage, as we all know, things are considerably different today.

Villages like Broadhembury and Gittisham are perfect examples of cob and thatch and a delight to the eye. The reasons for thatched roofs in Devon, in particular, is because they have less weight for the cob walls to carry. In Somerset things are very different, with beautiful Ham stone villages like Norton sub Hambdon and Montacute. Golden stone quarried for centuries from nearby Ham Hill, sunshine seems to release from it a store of light for it is one of those rare stones which, like Cotswold stone, varies in colour according to the weather.

Such was the manner in which the very rich lived their lives during the late eighteenth and early nineteenth century, that they were in complete ignorance of the dreadful conditions in which the artisans lived in their "charming country cottages", unaware of the slum conditions in which workers lived. The rich wanted to live the simple idyllic way, the way that they thought the average farm worker lived. So they built second homes, intending to live the simple life, with all the contemporary conveniences but without the squalor.

These desires coupled with the fact that the Napoleonic Wars had closed the great continental resorts to the upper classes, meant that such second homes were very often built at seaside resorts, place like Brighton, Torquay and Sidmouth.

The style they built in became known as "Cottage Orné", ornate cottages, the design of which was often taken out of "pattern" books, a sort of nineteenth century "Daily Mail Book of Houseplans". The most popular book at the time was J. C. London's "Encyclopaedia of Cottage, Farm and Villa Architecture".

Of all the South coast resorts Sidmouth, somehow, has managed to retain more unspoilt examples of "Cottage Orné" than other similar seaside towns. A perfect example is "The Royal Glen" hotel, formerly "Woolbrook Cottage," where Queen Victoria resided for a short while with her parents.

Sidmouth

Montacute
SOMERSET

It is generally accepted that the first Rural District Council Houses were built by Yeovil Rural District Council in 1912 at Townsend, Montacute near Yeovil in Somerset.

Fulfitt Terrace, as it is known, is constructed like the rest of the village in Hamstone – delightful houses with dormer windows. Several are now privately owned.

I spoke to Bert and Mabel Gaylard. Bert's mother and father were the first tenants when the rent was 3/6d (17^1/$_2$p) per week. Bert was born in the house in 1922 and has lived here ever since. The houses were built for £165 each.

Bert and Mabel are happy in the house although she admits to an occasional wish return to her birth place in Scotland.

Hallsands
DEVON

Man's greatest enemy, apart from himself, is the sea, which is, in turn, one of his greatest providers. So during the early sixteenth century the fishing village of Hallsands grew up on the South Devon coast, built on a substantial rock, harvesting the sea for the surrounding villages. All was well until 1896 when a licence was granted to take shingle to provide aggregate for the concrete extensions to Devonport Dockyard.

Two views of the ruins at Hallsands

Despite local protests that such excavations would reduce the level of the protective shingle beach, the government contractors, even more pitiless than the sea, removed three quarters of a million tons of gravel reducing the level of the beach by as much as nineteen feet. The resultant effect was disastrous. It exposed the village to the mercy of the sea and most of the cottages were swept away by the ferocious storms of 1917.

Virtually over night, a village, which in its time had boasted of a grocer's shop, post office, seamen's mission, piggery and public house, as well as homes for its 129 inhabitants, disappeared. Very little now remains of the village street, just bare rock; one cannot but admire the ingenuity of the builders who had cleverly used the narrow rock shelf as their foundations. Even now, parts of cottage walls are still standing, despite the fact that the supporting rocks continually suffer erosion. It's a sad indictment that we are, at the time of writing, precluded from going down to the beach as the path is too dangerous, threatened now by the cliffs as well as the sea. What a wicked lot we are and what a lot we have to answer for!

I've made a sketch of Hallsands as I think it would have looked in its heyday. The villagers had lived peacefully here for several centuries on the edge of the sea, literally on a shelf, the beach right up to their back gardens. They supplied the surrounding inland villages with fish in exchange for wheat and they had vegetables from their own tiny allotments. They were a self-contained unit with little need to travel, even as far as the nearest town. But as we have seen, almost overnight, the

village was swept away – all thirty houses – leaving the villagers homeless. Efforts were made to provide homes for them although the bureaucrats took their time, just as much as they do today. But that is another story. Suffice it to say that in the fullness of time, some compensation was paid and new homes built elsewhere.

Beesands
DEVON

But the story in no way finishes among these tragic ruins; far from it. Despite reassurances, back in 1924, that all was well with the sea bed, Beesands, a mile or so farther up the coast, suffered severe storm damage in both 1960 and 1980, which surely must be attributed to that dredging fiasco at the beginning of the present century. Unlike Hallsands, emergency measures were immediately implemented, and huge boulders were placed between the beach and the road, almost dwarfing the village.

Landlord of the Cricket Inn at Beesands, Cyril Courtenay, remembers the storms of 1960 and the beginning of the erosion, literally outside his front door. At that time the coastal defences were the responsibility of Kingsbridge Rural District Council. Although they were a small Council, they devised a scheme for a sea wall. This proved too expensive so huge boulders were used instead. Unfortunately the boulders gradually began to move, the sea undermining them, so more boulders were brought in. This lasted for several years until 1979, when a terrifying storm pulled the front to pieces, damaging the cottages. The Council and Water Authority, whose responsibility it now was, re-devised the sea wall. Whilst not the most beautiful of sights, the wall really does the job and Cyril and his fellow villagers can sleep secure in their beds, which was more than the inhabitants of Hallsands could, or did. Despite such setbacks, the village of Beesands has lived not just to fight another day, but also to welcome the many summer visitors who find their way to this remote part of South Devon.

Jolly Lane Cot, Hexworthy
DEVON

You might think that it is difficult to get planning permission on Dartmoor today: but to get permission to build a house was even more of a challenge in the nineteenth century. In 1832 a young couple, Tom and Sally Satterley, decided to get married.

However, their problem in providing a home was nothing like it is today, for it was a centuries-old custom rather than bureaucracy, which then ruled on Dartmoor. So what they did was to invoke one of the old moorland laws which said that any one able to build a house on common land, in a day – that was between sunrise and sunset – had the perpetual right of security for ever and could not be evicted. Such a privilege also allowed free grazing, fuel in the shape of peat and the gathering of bracken which was used for bedding.

Jolly Lane Cot at Hexworthy, near Princetown, is the house that Tom and Sally built, the last-known house ever to be built in a day. There was one major problem though; local farmers were violently opposed to "newcomers" taking up residence in this way. Tom, however, was no "newcomer", he was the ostler at the inn at Two Bridges and well used to moorland ways. With his

new bride, relations and friends, he hid sticks in a nearby ditch as well as hunks of granite for the walls and heather for the roof in the weeks before Ashburton Fair.

On the day of the event, after the local farmers had set off for the fair, Tom, Sally and companions built their house. They laboured for many hours, putting up this wonderful little one-storey house and by the time the farmers returned from the Fair, a fire was blazing in the hearth.

My sketch shows how the house would have looked. It was a primitive single storey building built with great lumps of granite, simple wooden windows

JOLLY LANE COTTAGE

and doorway. The roof was just long sticks covered in heather with dried gorse forming a sort of thatched roof. The chimney was just a hole in the middle. The idea of the ancient moorland law was that, if it was possible to light a fire on the hearth and for the smoke to be seen coming up through the hole in the roof, then the house was certainly yours.

Now, as you can see from the modern photograph, the house looks very different but if you look carefully you can still see, up to window sill level, the huge granite boulders originally used. They are so large at the corners you can almost feel their frenzy as they manoeuvred the ungainly slabs into position in order to beat both the clock and the setting sun. The house now has new windows and the timber lintels over the door have been superseded by those of brick. Another storey as been added and of course a new roof, a substantial roof, not at all like the one which Tom and Sally built.

Jolly Lane Cot had in its original form fulfilled all the Dartmoor regulations and was the last house in this lovely part of Dartmoor ever to do so. Sally, eighteen at the time the cottage was built, outlived her husband by about thirty-nine years and she spent sixty-nine years living happily in that simple house.

Not open to the public

Clovelly
NORTH DEVON

What a delight it is to find a complete village today totally unspoilt by time – no over head lines or other modern innovations like the motor car to ruin its appearance. Clovelly's amazing cobbled main street tumbles along the line of an old water course to the sea below. Still privately owned and carefully managed by the Rt. Hon. John Rous, it has successfully been able to maintain its old world character and charm. The sixteenth century cottages were restored and cleverly improved between 1914 and 1925 by former owner, Christine Hamblin, John Rous's aunt, whose initials still appear to be on many of the houses. Restoration work is indeed authentic and cob is once more being used. Because of difficulties, not only of access but because they are easier to handle, cob bricks are made on the site by Charlie, Ken and Edward, a team of master craftsmen. Obviously, transporting most items has been a problem in this

Clovelly, High Street, looking down

once busy fishing village, for donkeys carried, and still do for that matter, loads up the steep street, whilst sledges are used for the downward journey of goods. They also used to deliver beer to the New Inn at the top of the village – not an easy task!

Although Clovelly was recorded in the Domesday Book, George Cary, who died in 1601, is largely responsible for the layout of the village as we see it today. It was

NORTH HILL AND BACKSTAIRS, CLOVELLY.

built then at a cost of around £2,000. He was also responsible for the construction of the harbour, which was reconstructed later in 1795 and lengthened in 1826.

Clovelly offers the only anchorage for many miles, sheltered as it is from the prevailing South Westerly gales.

Whilst the village remains the same, people change. June, July and August see an influx of holiday makers who are welcomed to the village, up to seven thousand a day at the height of a season, attracting a total of some 300,000 visitors throughout the year.

Once a thriving fishing port, local fishermen still fish for herring, lobster and crab although income these days is slender, but the atmosphere of a fishing port is still captured around the bar of the local. The "Red Lion" pub was originally called the Jolly Sailor.

A former

Clovelly, Cottages on Beach

landlord was Robert Yeo, on whom Charles Kingsley, the writer, who grew up in the village, based one of his main characters in his famous novel "Westward Ho!" And, in a way, that seems to sum up the charm of this unique place – there is such a subtle blend of fact and fiction here that it's hard to differentiate between them.

Wesley's Cottage, Trewint
CORNWALL

Building materials tell us where we are. If it's flint then we are in East Anglia, in Somerset it is usually Ham Stone and in Devon, it is cob and thatch. In Cornwall we find the two strongest, most waterproof, materials of all – granite and slate. Whilst they are grey dull and inert they really are strong – given the chance they will last for ever. Smaller cottages, like the one at Trewint in Cornwall, are built of pieces of granite, whilst the bigger cottages required huge hunks, and both types have slate

roofs. But the dwelling at Trewint is no ordinary cottage, for John Wesley stayed here several times during his many evangelical missions bringing the Gospel to Cornwall. Banned from churches, he preached from natural Amphitheatres, huge grass circles such as Gwennap Pit.

Apparently, back in 1743, two of Wesley's agents, John Nelson and John Downes, came as an "advance party" to Cornwall. They had crossed Bodmin Moor and were tired, rain drenched, cold and miserable. They asked for refreshment at the little cottage at Trewint with its stone porch. It was owned by Digory Isbell and his wife Elizabeth, dedicated Church of England worshippers at the time who, being the good Samaritans that they were, put the two men up over night and fed them. Before leaving, the next morning, they got down on their knees and prayed at length "without a prayer book". This really impressed the Isbells and they learnt of their great leader, John Wesley. The Isbells converted to Methodism, like so many other Cornish people, and they welcomed Wesley on his first visit. So regular were the visits that Digory extended his cottage, providing on the first floor a "Prophet's chamber" for Wesley. The inspiration came from the Bible story of the

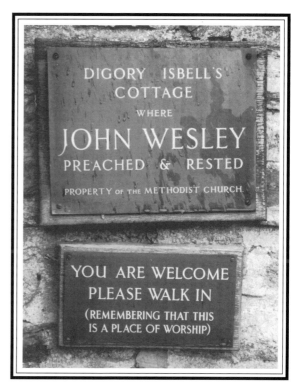

Shunamite women who built a "Prophet's chamber" for a man of God. The two room extension is a typically Cornish cottage in every way: a simple paving-stoned ground floor with a plain ceiling of planks resting on floor joists, forming the floor for the room above. There is a small fireplace and a considerable collection of bits and bobs, commemorating the thirty-two journeys which Wesley made into Cornwall, including pictures, candlesticks, hourglasses, and mementos of every sort.

I feel that there is something wonderful about places where famous people have either lived or visited. And there is a strong spiritual feeling in the upper room. This was the "Prophet's room". Throughout the years, people have donated various items including statues (one of him in his pulpit), china figures, plates, books, chalices, bibles and all sorts of commemorative pieces, all within simple white-washed walls as you would have found in cottages in those days, nothing expensive at all. A prize exhibit is a letter in Wesley's own handwriting, it gives you that "feeling of presence", enhanced by a notice that says: "Do not leave this upper room without a prayer for yourself and others." I picked up, downstairs, a copy of one of his short prayers, which I think is highly appropriate to the way we live our lives today: "God grant me the serenity to accept things I can not change, Courage to change the things I can, and Wisdom to know the difference." What lovely little prayer.

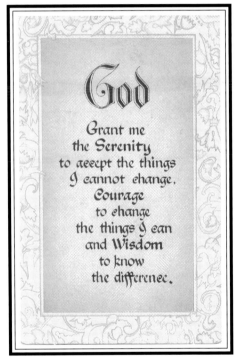

God

Grant me
the Serenity
to accept the things
I cannot change,
Courage
to change
the things I can
and Wisdom
to know
the difference.

···◆◉◗···

Two
CASTLES

A n Englishman's home is his castle," or so the old saying goes. This has to be true as, for untold centuries, man's worst enemy has been man himself. In order to protect his family and retainers, including his dogs and animals, he fortified his home – from the earliest cave dwellers who came home with dinner and rolled large stones across the entrance (the forerunner of our front door today I suppose), to the most sophisticated stronghold, the mediaeval castle. So his home became his castle.

Many such mediaeval castles survived the carnage of successive centuries and we think of them as romantic places, castles complete like Windsor or alternatively attractive ruins like Corfe in Dorset, one of the castles Cromwell "knocked about a bit". But the very earliest castles were much simpler than their grandiose successors.

As my grandson Thomas is better at making sandcastles than me, I called him in to give some "expert" advice on building a traditional sandcastle. It is surprising how similar they are to the very early Norman Motte and Bailey castles built after the Conquest in 1066. As there are so very few of these basically simple castles left for us to see today, I built my own scaled down version on Sidmouth beach. As you can see from the photograph the high Motte was where the Lord and his Lady lived whilst servants, serfs and animals used the lower Bailey. The Normans built in excess of six hundred such castles. All the buildings were of timber and the high bank surrounding the castles above the moat had a timber palisade. As they were built mostly of timber, it is not surprising that little remains to be seen today.

Corfe Castle
DORSET

However much later Motte and Bailey castles were built in stone, Corfe Castle in Dorset being an almost perfect example. A National Trust property, open to the public, this ruin dominates the Purbeck landscape, protruding on its Motte like a badly worn tooth; but the comparison fades as you get nearer for this has to be one of the most glorious ruins.

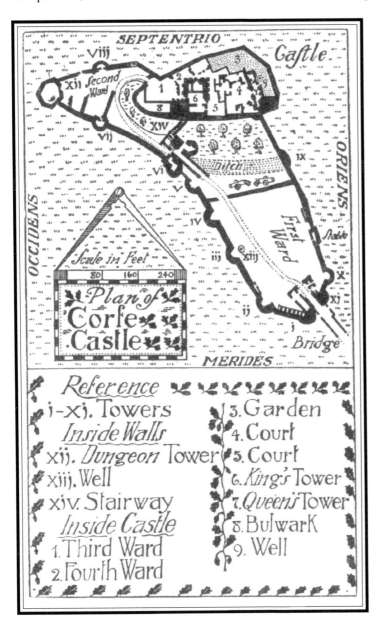

At one time a Royal residence, it survived centuries of conflict only to be slighted by Cromwell during the Civil War. Having been held for three years against the Cromwellians, by just thirty men under the leadership of Lady Bankes, it was finally taken through treachery by one of the thirty, who opened the postern gate, letting in the Roundheads. Although undamaged during the conflict, Cromwell ordered it to be destroyed, which explains why the ruins look as they do today.

However there is an opportunity to see it as it was in its heyday, for in

A plan of Corfe Castle, drawn in 1903.

the village there is a one-twentieth scale model located nearby in a garden in Corfe, showing the castle as it looked before it was slighted. You can see clearly

The village of Corfe, as it looked c. 1900

the defensive situation, the outer moat, with banks on either side, and a curtain wall which has half round towers at regular intervals. The wall continues

unbroken all the way round, dropping down below the Motte, on top of which stands the Great Keep. When the castle was under attack all the villagers came into the lower Bailey bringing their cattle and belongings with them.

The weakest point of any castle was the gatehouse, so this had to be the most strongly defended. Had they indeed broken through, they would

have been faced by a row of canon at the bottom of the bank below the Keep. Had they silenced these then they were faced with yet another inner Gatehouse, which provided access to the main keep.

It is thought that Corfe, one of Edward I's castles, was initially built for something like £7,000, that is about 45 pence per foot (in old pence as well!) taking one thousand men four years to construct.

It is not common knowledge that castle walls were painted in various bright colours outside. They took on the colours of the Duke or Knight who owned the castle, taking them from his standard and applying them to the walls. They usually painted the battlement red for the simple reason that blood stains would not show up, frightening the defenders. Soldiers wore red jackets for much the same reason in later years. If the walls weren't coloured then they were whitewashed both inside and out. Orders to whitewash Corfe still survive in Chaucer's words, "Long Castell with walles white."

What a glorious sight it must have been.

Powderham Castle
DEVON

I was received by Lord Courtenay, on the terrace of his superb castle, surrounded by his dogs. He is justifiably proud of the fact that the castle has been in his family for about six hundred years. The original castle was built by the family between 1390 and 1420, and was sympathetically enlarged in the eighteenth and nineteenth centuries. What a heritage the family has! It must be a purer lineage even than our Royal Family, whose line we know has been broken more than once over the centuries.

The family originally came over from France in the twelfth century with branches living in various parts of the country. The branch who came to Powderham, and which Lord Courtenay describes as a "junior" branch, survived the Wars of the Roses, which destroyed the "senior" branch of the family. The French side of the family finally died out altogether with several Courtenays settling in Ireland, and eventually on to America where there are still Courtenays today.

The castle has been added to over the years. It has remained much in its original form from 1420 until the time of the Civil War when it was badly damaged by the

Cromwellian forces. The family then moved out for about seventy years, returning to rebuild the damaged castle, very largely during the eighteenth century, remodelling it at the same time.

Lord Courtenay showed me his favourite room, the enchanting music room, which is one of the rooms added on to the castle in the 1790s. Designed by architect James Wyatt, it has glorious Italian marble columns and a splendid fireplace, designed by one of the finest designers of the time, Richard Westmacott. Constructed of Carera marble, it is contemporary with the room. I wonder how they managed, at that time, to bring down to the remote West Country one of the top architects? Lord Courtenay thinks it was because they probably paid him extremely well! All the wall colours are as they would have been at the time; the ceiling is actually in its original paint and colours, although the walls and dome have been repainted. There are carvings of musical instruments around the top and a superb chandelier, which has never been converted to a modern utility but still uses candles. The delicately patterned Axminster carpet, by Thomas Whitty, is probably one of the best preserved carpets of the period still in existence.

The magnificent organ is actually older than the room. It is thought that the room had a stage in the position it now occupies.

The wonderful staircase is considered to be the most sumptuous example of Rococo architecture in the country. It is late Baroque in conception with leaves, animals and plants all spilling out over the frames. This wonderfully ornate plaster work was carried out by a local craftsman, John Jenkins, back in 1754. Like many builders he underestimated his quote for £214 and 4 shillings. When the final bill came it was for £355. The lord at that time was not too happy. However he must have been pacified, for he ordered the splendid Coat of Arms at the bottom of the staircase, which cost an extra £4. The sea green wall colouring is subtly graded, from top to bottom.

So many of our stately homes have been separated from their "families" or have been taken over by the state in lieu of taxation over the years. I asked Lord Courtenay if he had a special secret which allowed him to maintain Powderham as a home? He told me that it is very difficult to keep going and he has been taxed like everyone else. He agreed with me that heavy taxation seems to be a strange penalty to inflict on people struggling to maintain their, and the nation's, heritage. It is a 'no win' situation; in order to pay taxes you have to sell heirlooms and if you do that, then you are attacked by the establishment for disposing of the nation's treasures – a situation suffered by many dedicated people like Lord Courtenay. The sooner, to put it crudely, the government of the day "pulls its finger out" to help them, the better it will be and national treasures like Powderham Castle will be secured for ever.

Sherborne Castles
DORSET

Sherborne, in Dorset, has the advantage of having not only one but two castles. The old Norman castle sadly is now in ruins, another of those that Cromwell "knocked about a bit" and these proud ruins gaze across the lake autocratically at the "newer" castle, a mere four hundred years old!

The house was originally built for Sir Walter Raleigh, who is reputed to have seen the old castle whilst riding from Plymouth to London saying "that's for me," or words to that effect. It was not quite as easy as that for the castle was the summer residence of the Bishop of Salisbury. Raleigh, a past master at intrigues, bribed Queen Elizabeth I with a £250 trinket (at today's values something in the region of a quarter of a million) she "relieved" the Bishop of his "holiday home" and leased it to Raleigh on a ninety-nine year lease for two hundred and one pounds and a penny! It proved difficult and expensive to adapt for his needs so he decided to develop a small hunting lodge across the lake, the nucleus of the "new" castle today.

The old castle ruins before the vegetation was removed

Raleigh's finished new castle was much smaller than it is today. Wings were later added by the new owners, the Digby family who still own the property and whose home it has been up until this century. What is remarkable is that the castle survived the Civil War, when in 1645 Cromwell and General Fairfax, arrived at Sherborne with their main army.

It was arranged to spare the castle, through the intervention of Lady Digby who was formerly a Bedford herself, and Bedford was an important figure on the parliamentary hierarchy.

No such luck for the old castle, it was too well fortified so Cromwell slighted it, with a vengeance!

Situated in magnificent parkland, the castle's setting is delightful. Deer roam freely in the park, designed by Capability Brown, and it is a rare delight to gaze upon from just about any window in the castle.

On my visit to the castle I was fortunate enough to be personally welcomed by the present owner, Mr Simon Wingfield Digby. We sat and talked in his favourite room, the red drawing room, which used to be his father's study. He is particularly proud of the fact that the house has been in his family for four hundred years and counts himself "an extraordinarily lucky chap". He remembers his childhood during the First World War when the Castle was requisitioned and used as a hospital. The wounded soldiers were kind to the boys, digging trenches for them, making wooden rifles and teaching them the kind of tactics used in the First World War. He also recalls how lovely the grounds were for playing, and the two tunnels under the courtyard, where the boys would play fox and hounds trying to cut off "the fox" as he came out of the tunnel!

Hanging in this magnificent red drawing room is perhaps one of the most famous historical pictures ever painted, and found in all the history books – a picture of Queen Elizabeth I in a procession of some magnificence.

There appear to be many differing theories about what is happening in the painting. The main point is that she is not being carried on a litter at all but is being wheeled along in a wheel barrow! The procession never actually took place but was a sort of propaganda in support of some of the leading families after the death of Essex. Apart from the Knights of the Garter, the picture depicts all the prominent figures during the end of the reign of Queen Elizabeth.

If the red drawing room is Simon Wingfield Digby's favourite room, then mine must be the dining room, for all sorts of reasons. You enter by way of an indoor porch, a brilliant idea, and a good way to keep out the draughts, much more satisfactory than our external porches today, beautifully carved with egg and dart motifs and other Renaissance detail. The dining room is a superb room enhanced for me by the long, imposing dining table. It is made out of two sections of oak, in order to get it through the door! The fireplace, almost big enough to roast an ox, has a crack in one of the paving slabs. Who apart from myself would be fascinated by such a crack? Apparently it was made by the weight of the printing press used by William of Orange, personally, when he stayed at Sherborne for three days on his way to London. The original proclamation, in which he declared himself King of England, was printed here.

Simon Wingfield Digby regrets being unable to actually live in the house today, mainly because it would be virtually impossible to find sufficient staff to run it as a home. In his youth there would have been fifteen or more full time staff including grooms as well as outside staff one of whom, I was pleased to tell Mr Wingfield Digby, had been my grandfather, a master mason.

The good news is that Simon Wingfield Digby has a son and heir to the house, so there is every hope that it will remain in the caring hands of the Digby family for at least another four hundred years.

Barley Splatt, Graham Ovenden's Castle
CORNWALL

"An Englishman's home is his castle" and yet most of us live in a "three up and two downer". Not internationally-acclaimed artist Graham Ovenden though; his castle is his home. He is building his very own unique twentieth century castle, near Mount, in the depths of Cornwall. Graham has already been working on his castle, almost single-handed, for twenty years and he estimates it will take him another twenty years before he completes it. Built in the style of a baronial hall, the design of the house is nineteenth century in concept and described by Graham as "polychromatic Gothic"

or more accurately, as he puts it, "geometric Gothic". Graham is half-Cornish himself and most of his family came from the West Country, so he has actually returned to his roots. Apart from writing and painting, he also has a great interest in architecture and nineteenth century applied arts. From an early age he was aware of great nineteenth century architects like William Burgess, Pugin and George Edmund Street, and of Victorian designers like Owen Jones. He was brought up with a generation of people who could meet people like Nikolaus Pevsner and John Betjeman.

Graham has done most of the building work himself and has his own granite cutting machine. He believes that it is important to use indigenous materials and has used polychromatic granites and different coloured slates.

The partially completed castle is glorious, a fun building, with serious overtones. Built around the nucleus of an ancient and simple Cornish cottage, which has now been absorbed and is encased in granite, this has enlarged, rather than destroyed it. The little cottage has become part of the actual castle.

Many different types of stone have been used, 95 per cent of the building is constructed from local granites using indigenous materials, with Delabole slate and marble used for ornamentation. It is as much as anything a celebration of local geology.

The interior is quite wonderful and the theme continues throughout the castle. It was conceived on all four points of the compass so that when you walk round there are no

blank surfaces either inside or out.

The next stage of this "Gothic Castle" will be the building of the main central tower, with castellations on top of the walls, followed by the construction of the final wing. This will form the grand entrance hall, a true baronial hall, which will go up to the full roof height and have a gallery and staircase giving access to the upper part of the building.

One man's inspired ambition to truly create something for himself has already become an enviable little paradise for himself and his family to enjoy.

Not open to the public

Trago Mills, Newton Abbot
DEVON

Trago Mills at Newton Abbot looks like a fairy tale castle, complete with towers, turrets, grotesques and white-washed throughout. It is no castle however but, would you believe it, a modern hypermarket! It is what I like to call "fun architecture" and what a pity we do not see more like it. There is no precedent for the design of such a complex, so why shouldn't it look like a castle? Sadly contemporary architecture is split into two schools of thought. On one extreme we have modern buildings with all their insides in the shape of service pipes, heating ducts even the main structural frame, cluttering up the outside for all to see – buildings like the Pompidou Centre in Paris. On the other side we have Prince Charles and his followers supporting traditional architecture. Right in the middle is "fun" architecture, buildings like Trago Mills "cocking a snook" at both sides and not only enjoying it themselves but giving us a chuckle as well.

David Young 'rescues' Nicky Booth – a maiden from the tower!

Let's have more fun buildings like this – who knows perhaps the idea may catch on. Well done Trago Mills!

···—◉—···

❧ *Three* ❧
PUBS

No other building, apart from the Parish Church, illustrates the social history of this country better than the pub. For a thousand or more years, it has been a common meeting place where the mighty quenched their thirst and rubbed shoulders with the lowest in the land whilst partaking of a pint of ale. For a moment all men are equal. The origin of the pub stemmed from the building of the Parish Churches. It was rarely built by local labour instead groups of itinerant craftsmen, masons, wood carvers and stained glass designers, who travelled together as a team, did the work. They would move from village to village building the Parish Churches. The first thing they did was to build themselves a sort of mediaeval "portacabin", usually a simple structure of stone and thatch where they could live and sleep whilst they were carrying out the work. It often took three or four years to build such churches so somewhere nearby to stay was imperative. At the end of that period they just simply packed up and left, just moved out leaving the building empty, until one or two local bright sparks in the community put their heads together, and said "let's turn this into a pub" and that is exactly what happened.

The relationship between church and pub is beautifully illustrated in John Betjeman's book "Church Poems". It was one of his favourites and is one of mine. It's called "Churchyards"

"For churchyards then on hallowed ground
Were not so grim as now they sound.
And horns of ale were handed round
For which Church wardens used to pay
On each especial vestry day.
'Twas thus the village drinks its beer
(with its relations buried near.)
And that is why we often see,
Inns where the alehouse used to be,
Close to the church where prayers were said,
And masses for the village dead."

Church House Inn, Rattery
SOUTH DEVON

The Church House Inn at Rattery in South Devon dates from the eleventh century and records go back that far. The craftsmen who built the church were often monks as well and enthusiastic landlord Brian Evans has a list of clergy from that time. He has carried out a great deal of research and even has the names of landlords back to 1603. During that period of time, right up until today, there have only been twenty-five landlords, a number slightly less than the vicars. He even has the census returns for 1841 and 1851 and is surprised at the amount of information they contain. For instance, the Coaker family had the pub for one hundred years, as families did not move around much as they do today.

The pub is listed as an ancient monument and Brian has to retain its original character. There is a wonderful old timber screen at one end. People from all over the world come to see this marvellous old place, a genuine and virtually unspoilt "Church House Inn".

Pack o' Cards Inn, Combe Martin
NORTH DEVON

Great Britain abounds with architectural follies and there would seem to be more in the West Country than anywhere else in the country, but not all follies were impractical buildings. One of the most practical, in many people's opinion, is the "Pack O' Cards Inn" at Combe Martin in North Devon. Its claim to fame is that it looks exactly like a house of cards, for it was built to commemorate a win at cards. Local squire, George Ley, an inveterate gambler, chanced his family fortune and estates on the turn of a card, swearing that if he won, he would never gamble again but would build a dwelling to look like a pack of cards. The card turned in his favour, he won a fortune and spent it constructing a most

unusual house, which became a pub. It was certainly the work of an eccentric, as there are four floors to correspond with the number of suits, thirteen doors on each floor, to match the number of cards in a suit, and fifty-two windows. It's fifty-two feet square and fifty-two feet high, all matching the number of cards in a pack.

with brandy or rum as a base. This drink is also mentioned in Dickens' books and in "Martin Chuzzlewit." The young Martin, on arriving in America, was given "Sherry Cobbler", oranges, sherry, port and a little sugar! The book is full of many more exciting drinks which I am sure would cost a fortune to make at today's prices!

Cedric insists that he was born and bred as a teetotaller. His French grandmother did not count wine as an alcoholic drink as it was an important drink with meals, so he was allowed to drink wine, well watered. She did not count brandy because brandy was kept in the medicine cupboard, so it 'wasn't alcohol'! Every time he was on the verge of or about to get a cold, along came the hot toddy and his grandmother always put the brandy in last so as not to lose any of the alcohol. What a wonderful way to cure a cold and of course Cedric assures me that he had a lot of colds as a small boy!

It was through Cedric that I learnt a lot about the "Tiddly Winks" pubs of Victorian times. A government decree said that any householder could sell beer, but not spirits, upon paying £2 a year licence. People really only drank beer or gin from the pubs and even children drank beer because water was so undrinkable. One wonders how long it will be before our children will have to resort to beer once more, though I don't think we will ever again see gin at 2 pence a bottle!

I had found, in a sale, a paperback copy of "Martin Chuzzlewit". Many of the earliest Dickens novels were published in pamphlets, in serial form and my 'find' was one of the very first ones. Brought out in monthly parts the novels were usually in twenty parts, surely the first "soap" and people in America would receive their copies long after Britain had read them and would be impatiently waiting at the quay for the next instalment. My copy is No 7 so there would have been six parts before and twelve afterwards to make a set. A complete set of these, Cedric told me, would be worth a small fortune today. I was delighted when Cedric signed it for me on behalf of his famous relative. I shall certainly treasure my very own signed copy with its special quote from "Mr Micawber" and written in by Cedric.

"David old fellow you and me always were good friends"!

That we are Cedric!

Pub Signs

With much of the population illiterate it is not surprising that signs illustrating their wares were put up by tradesmen in mediaeval times. The butcher, the baker and candlestick maker all had hanging signs. For some inexplicable reason, the only hanging signs to have survived until today are those of the pub and the red and white barber's pole, although few of these can be found today. The alternate red and white,

indicated the barber surgeon – fortunately the days of a close back and sides and a quick bleeding have long since gone.

The earliest pub sign was a bunch of vines and ivy tied onto a pole outside the Roman wine shops. The "Bush" is still in use today, as a pub sign. "The Bush" at Morwenstow in Cornwall can boast of such a sign, as well as being one of the country's oldest pubs, it has stood there for over one thousand years.

Whilst we have seen that many pubs started life as "workmen's huts" put up and used by travelling craftsmen, others developed as pubs when, after the Dissolution of the Monasteries, Henry VIII held on to the Monastery guest houses, allowing them to be converted to pubs, the "George and Pilgrim" at Glastonbury in Somerset, being a fine example. Many "Kings Heads" stem from that time, the creeps! Signs then fell into categories: heraldic signs where publicans adopted the arms of local families – the "Phelips Arms" at Montacute in Somerset, the "Drewe Arms" at Broadhembury in Devon; trade signs like the "Butchers Arms" and the "Glovers Arms" both at Yeovil in Somerset; and Patriotic signs – "The Duke of York" and the "Battle of Waterloo". One such sign celebrating a successful war with the Spanish was the "Infantile de Castle," which by way of a misunderstanding became phonetically correct but wrongly translated as "Elephant and Castle". Similarly the sign "God Encompasses Us" became "Goat and Compasses". Sports are catered for with pubs like "The Cricket Inn" at Beesands or the "Greyhound" in Yeovil in Somerset. Many of the "New Inns" took the name of the time when Charles II was restored to the throne. In

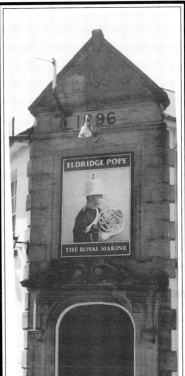

much the same way as pubs took on the name of coaches during the early eighteenth century, like "The Quick Silver Mail" in Yeovil, so in latter parts of the nineteenth century they celebrated the coming of the railway with names like "The Great Western". We are brought up to date with a truly modern sign in a London pub "The Satellite".

No mention of pubs is complete without mention of the place the beer comes from. Palmers Brewery, the only brewery with a thatched roof, is one of the very few still in family ownership. It celebrated its bicentenary in 1994 and a new beer "Palmers 200" was launched in celebration.

The brewery was established in 1794 by Samuel Grundy, and was taken over by the Palmer family. Brothers, John and Cleeves Palmer run the brewery and they have a highly skilled team of forty-five employees. Brewing is an art in itself and the team

need to understand the raw materials and how to measure them, how to evaluate and make sure that every pint served from the cask is exactly the same quality.

Cleeves Palmer explained the process to me: Spring water, called liquor in a brewery, is taken from a supply nearby and pumped into a holding tank, boiled and added to malted barley. The first process is to mash together the barley and water, extracting the malt extract from the grains. The mixture is then sent up to a copper where hops are added. It is then boiled vigorously, giving that wonderful bitterness and aroma which adds flavour to the beer, which is then chilled down to the correct temperature of 60 degrees Fahrenheit and fermented for seven days.

The thatched brewery is compact enough for conducted parties to watch the fascinating brewing process from start to finish and parties are shown around by appointment.

I feel sure that the caring Palmer family will continue to produce fine ales in this delightful Dorset thatched brewery for at least another two hundred years.

I love pubs for many reasons, not least because of what one gets inside, not just a good pint of beer, but even more the history that is connected with them. At the George Hotel at West Bay near Bridport in Dorset, Oliver and I had the privilege and pleasure of performing a rare ceremony, the unveiling of a brand new pub sign. Commissioned by Palmers Brewery, and painted by sign painter Ken Allen of Yeovil, it is after Sir Thomas Lawrence's famous painting of George IV. Ken's magnificent portrait hangs majestically gazing out over West Bay harbour to the sea.

Ken Allen started painting pub signs after a chance meeting with famous Bridport sign painter, George Biles, an artist who painted signs for some seventy-three years prior to his death some seven years ago. Ken learnt the tricks of the trade from George, always following his advice and drawing on his experience; in fact he still bases some of his designs on George's originals. Ken usually starts with a pencil sketch drawing, associating it with the name of the pub. For instance the "Plymouth Inn" has the Arms of the City on one side and Sir Francis Drake on the other. Ken proudly points out that his signs will last for twenty or twenty-five years with the simplest of maintenance, merely an annual wash, polish and buff.

How splendid it is to see someone like Ken Allen following in the footsteps of an old master craftsman such as George Biles.

Normandy Arms, Blackawton
DEVON

The Normandy Arms at Blackawton in South Devon has a fine collection of paraphernalia relevant to D-Day. On display is a copy of the powerful message which General Eisenhower sent to everyone under his command on the eve of D-Day. Next to it is General Montgomery's equivalent message. Strong, stirring stuff, full of powerful images similar to the St Crispin's Day Speech by Henry V, and rousing stuff at that. There are many photographs of the main contenders including Monty and Eisenhower, of course. There are even hand painted portraits of them, painted by a local artist who also does pub signs here in the South Hams. Many of the leaders, as

well as other ranks, used the pub during the war, hence its name. In one corner hangs a raincoat, not any old raincoat, it is said to be the one left by General Eisenhower, as he rushed off to D-Day. He was the one above all others who knew the actual date, so why should he, of all people, have moved off in such a hurry, leaving his coat? Still it is a good story, perhaps an omen and let's hope it will be hanging there in forty years time, undisturbed by any further conflicts!

Chris Wills, a regular at the pub who lives in the village remembers how the whole area was evacuated to accommodate American troops practising for D-Day, an operation known as "Exercise Tiger". He was living with his Grandmother at the time

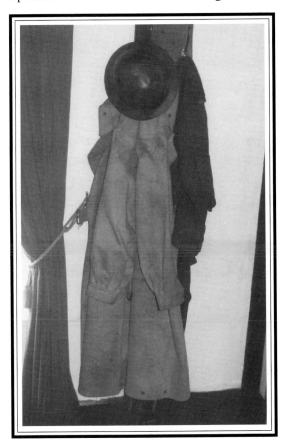

that they were told of the D-Day rehearsals and the need to evacuate their homes. They were moved in horse and carts to outlying areas, with families sharing houses for about eighteen months. He well remembers the Americans passing in their trucks and throwing chocolate to him and the other boys as they left. Returning to their homes, some families found their houses in a bad shape – holes in the kitchen walls where dart boards had hung – and some of the doors even had bullet holes in them, but on the whole they had been well looked after by the troops.

Although it was hushed up at the time and news did not leak out until years later, one of the rehearsals fell foul of a German raiding party. Chris tells the story in his own words: "When they did the rehearsal for the raid on Slapton Beach all the boats were there and landing craft with the soldiers coming in when suddenly some German E boats crept up, slipped in amongst them, whipped off a few torpedoes and blew them up. There were a lot of soldiers killed who were reputed to have been buried in big mass grave. Rumour has it that something like a thousand men were killed and the bodies transported by the lorry load. However, no such grave has been found. They have a memorial to this event on Slapton Sands which is now, of course, a tourist attraction. Ken Small from Torcross discovered an American tank in the sea, a year or two ago, winched it out of the water, put it onto a plinth and painted it, so we have yet another tourist attraction which stands proudly by the side of Slapton Ley at Torcross, a very different type of memorial to all those who lost their lives there."

••• ➤●◉●➤ •••

∽ *Four* ∽
CHURCHES

You might think that I'm really stretching a point when I say that our parish churches are our only link with the Roman occupation. In fact we can go back even further for very often churches were built on pagan sites, many of them earth circles, dating from prehistoric times. They were adopted by Christian missionaries simply because such sites were established meeting places, albeit to observe pagan rites. Such familiarity greatly helped missionaries to convert our early ancestors away from their pagan gods to Christianity.

Colyton Church

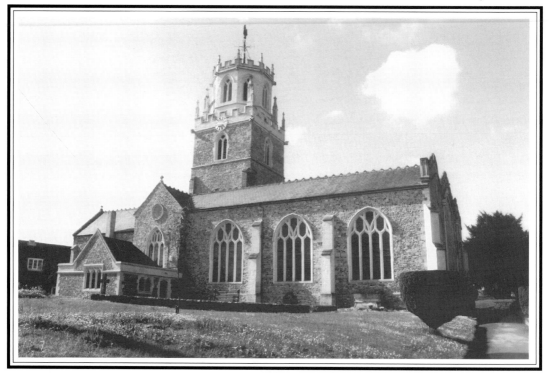

Colyton Parish Church
EAST DEVON

The Lantern Tower of St Andrew's Parish Church in Colyton in East Devon has played its part over the centuries, guiding seafarers to safe haven. There is, however, a more prosaic reason for this fine tower in so far that it was inspired by similar towers in Flanders; towers which would have been familiar to the town's wool merchants. This seems to be more than a possibility, as they gave some of their profits towards the building of the church in grateful thanks to the Lord for their prosperity. Good money, well spent, created some wonderful churches during the late mediaeval times, of which St Andrew's is such a fine example.

Folk go into a church today, look around and say, "Isn't that a lovely bit of stone work" or "Isn't that rendering nice?" But what they do not realise is that in mediaeval times the whole place was ablaze with colour – the entire church was illuminated like a jewel box. The walls and roof were painted in blues and reds, as well as the tombs, the altar, even the font, everything. This church has been restored a number of times over the years with most restorers attempting to retain some of the original colours. The Pole chapel with its ornate tombs shows the vivid use of colour in the architecture of the church. Stone painted to look like marble was common at the time. There is a magnificent tomb where the man and wife are lying back to back looking as if they had fallen out! It looks a most uncomfortable position and I feel sure resurrection day would have come as a relief to both of them! There is one very small tomb, apparently a child's tomb, with all sorts of legends attached to it. The rector, the Reverend David Gunn-Johnson, has a great affection for the church and he told me that the tiny tomb, one of the smallest in the country, was that of Margaret, the daughter of Edward IV, who died choking on a fish bone at Calcombe Castle; hence the legend of "Little-choke-a-bone". However, later research ruined the story for on the tomb there are three shields, proving she was a married woman. In the original colours the shield on the right hand side had a blue and silver border, around the Royal Arms, which made it a Beaufort shield. So it was necessary to search for a Beaufort who married a Courtenay and in 1431, Margaret Beaufort married a Courtenay and there are no recorded facts as to how she died or why the tomb is so small. What a shame it is when all these fascinating legends get killed off by modern research.

Oliver accompanied me into the church and I of course had him on a lead, but in mediaeval times, right up to 1850, dogs were welcome in church and roamed freely so the altar rail was erected for a practical purpose – to prevent dogs "misbehaving" themselves in the altar area! That did not stop them performing elsewhere in the church so a new post was created, that of a "Dog Whipper". His duty was to rush around the church "whipping out" the dogs. Can you imagine it? What a sight, worthy of a "Tom and Jerry" cartoon. Later, when dogs were eventually banned, it was decided that the children were just as obnoxious, so the post was retained and he was renamed "Child Whipper" !

Church windows took on the colour of the walls and to the average mediaeval worshipper who could neither read nor write imagery was all important. When he came into the church, he was entering a symbolic universe. The nave represented "Earth", and his first glimpse of heaven was the nave roof, with its painted angels and

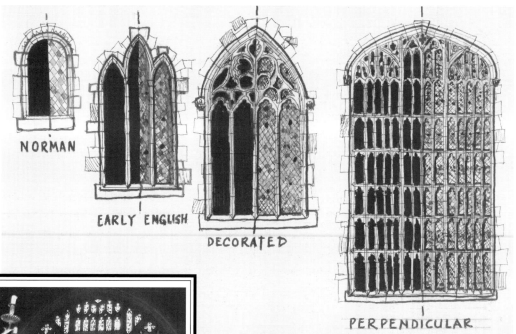

NORMAN

EARLY ENGLISH

DECORATED

PERPENDICULAR

stars, a celestial heaven. Uneducated as he was he relied on the priest for information. He was in the Chancel, known as "Heaven". To strive to get there he had to pass through the barrier of death, which was symbolised by the arch between the Chancel and the nave. Life ever after was again symbolic, the crucified Christ, either fixed above the Chancel arch or on a rood screen, together with his mother Mary and St John.

It is not common knowledge that what we know as Gothic architecture was not broken up into periods and separate styles until 1817 when an architectural archaeologist, Thomas Rickman, straightened up some five hundred years of confusion. He divided Gothic into four styles, or as some people prefer it today, "stages of evolution".

My drawing opposite shows this. Norman (1066–1189) with its simple round arch, unusually narrow and small. Glass was hardly known at the time so sheets of shale or hide were used instead. Early English (1189–1307) identified the narrow pointed arch, often known as lancet. Some experts think "lancets" may have come from two rounded arches interlocking. Decorated (1307–1377) was much more ornate. Wool merchants often gave money to build chapels where regular mass could be said for their departed souls. It was their endowments which inspired craftsmen to take more time producing delicate carvings and flamboyant tracery. For me there is nothing grander than the Perpendicular (1377–1485) and the West window in this church is the most glorious example, probably the biggest in any parish church in the country. It is a great mass of glass broken up by small mullions and transoms, quite magnificent and a delight to see.

Colyton can boast of not only beautiful ancient stained glass but a really "modern stained glass" window as well. During an all night, Maundy Thursday, vigil about seventy young people from the town made a complete stained glass window, an Easter representation. A golden cross rising out of the sun, with the tree of life alongside, made of bits of coloured plastic welded together. How wonderful to think of today's East Devon young folk bringing colour, craftsmanship and above all the love of one another, once again into their lovely church.

Barnstaple Parish Church
NORTH DEVON

For me our beautiful churches are incomplete without music. Sit in any church pew and you will find something missing in the ambience of the place. It is as if the architecture is frozen music which is released the moment the organ is played; in much the same way as our prayers seem to release those of previous generations stored over the centuries in the fabric, to join our own.

I had this experience when world-renowned organist, Jennifer Bate, played so brilliantly especially for us at Barnstaple Parish Church. The organ, recently restored, has as fascinating a history as the Church itself. I cannot do better than to quote from the Church's excellent guidebook:

"The present organ was installed in 1764. It stood on a low gallery at the West End of the church and was originally surmounted by enormous gilt angels! The organ was built by the Crang family and presented to the Church by Sir George Amyand, one of the town's MP's and a friend of the composer G. F. Handel. In 1872 the organ was

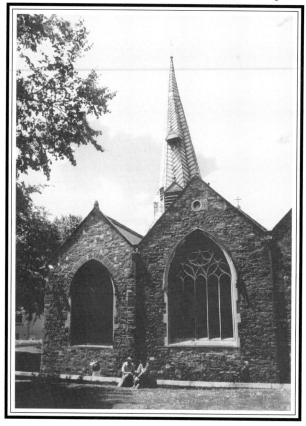

partly renovated and moved to a position between the North Transept and the North Chancel aisle. More renovations took place in 1916 and 1938 but since then the instrument has been slowly deteriorating. It was decided in 1991 to go ahead with all the necessary repairs to bring the organ back to its former glory and to move it once again, this time to an open position in the North Transept, where it will be seen and heard so much better from the body of the Church. Work commenced on 20th April 1992 and was completed on 10th November, at a cost of nearly £100,000. The organ was rededicated by the Bishop of Crediton on 18 November 1992."

Bearing in mind today's costs it is interesting to find that the original

Jennifer Bate

fifteenth century organ was repaired back in 1497 by "Mr Thomas, organ player" for the sum of 9s.2d. (46p) a princely sum no doubt in those days.

The Church was badly damaged by fire in 1793 and struck by lightning in 1810 when amongst other damage the weather cock, on top of the Church's distinctive broach spire, melted! When Victorian Church architect Sir Gilbert Scott made a survey he said it was unsafe and should be demolished and completely rebuilt. However he was persuaded to restore it and his skilful efforts surround us today.

The Church's greatest treasures survived better than the rest of the fabric, the windows lighting a glorious interior, an experience which, as I said earlier, is completed for me by the organ music.

Warleggan Church
CORNWALL

Cornish eccentrics do not only belong to the past for, as recently as 1950 there was a vicar of the tiny parish church, at Warleggan, tucked away on the edge of Bodmin moor, who was a wild eccentric and who became a recluse. The present vicar, the Reverend Tony Olivey, told me about the Reverend George Densham who had taken the living at Warleggan in 1931. A well-educated man, well versed in Greek, Latin and Hebrew, he found himself desperately lonely in this out-of-the-way spot. With little to do, he became a little unbalanced, quickly alienating his parishioners by his strange ways. He took services at odd times, matins at six o'clock in the morning instead of eleven, evensong at two thirty and other services at strange times. The parishioners complained strongly to the Bishop and Archdeacon, but there was little they could do and his congregation soon diminished. The service records are still in the church. One entry for 1951 reads "No rain, no wind, no sun, no congregation". During the whole of that year only 31 people in all attended services and most of those were Densham himself. The church collections for that year totalled eleven shillings and threepence donated by himself, no doubt.

Such were the complaints that the Reverend Densham was in danger of losing his

living altogether, and he was so upset at the lack of congregations that he made cardboard cut-out figures and placed them in the pews!

He was very much the architect of his own demise. Having alienated himself from the community by his strange ways, he became a recluse turning his house, the vicarage, into a fortress. He dug a moat around it, put up a twelve foot high fence and bought at least a dozen dogs that ran loose all the time. He was rarely seen after that. Apparently Daphne Du Maurier came, with a friend, to try and visit him. The friend clambered to the top of the fence, saw Densham and called out. He took one look at her and ran into the vicarage. That was the last time he was ever seen alive. About six months later, for he had not been seen for several weeks, someone broke into the house. The dogs were starving and the Reverend Densham was found dead at the bottom of the stairs.

It is a sad tale really; a sad end of a man who was academically brilliant, who ended up preaching to a congregation of cardboard cutouts. I am sure he would be envious of the numbers of parishioners who regularly attend the little moorland church for services nowadays!

Former rectory not open to the public

Tawstock Church

NORTH DEVON

Tawstock church in North Devon is rich in tombs and monuments, containing probably more than any other parish church comparable in size. Whether rich or poor you made your last journey in the village bier. It is a glorified trolley really on which the coffin was brought in to the church. The graves of the earliest people buried in the church were covered by flat tombstones containing their names. Priests usually had a chalice carved on their tombstones, whilst a knight had a sword. They were buried facing the East so that

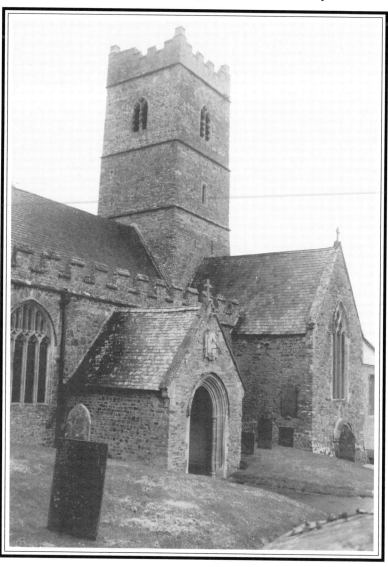

they were ready for resurrection day, except the poor old priest who, because of his office, was facing the congregation. The clergy realising that they could make money out of burials in church, charged a fiver a time, which was of course an enormous amount of money back in mediaeval times. Because it was such a moneymaking occupation they became greedy, and packed too many people in. Burials were on three levels and in many early churches the tragedy was that final burials were only about two feet below the floor and the stench of decaying corpses came up through the

floor boards causing illness amongst the congregation, so rosemary, frankincense and fragrances were scattered about.

Understandably they dropped the idea of burying people in that way and seized upon another good way of making money by putting in rather ornate tombs like the one of the Earl and Countess of Bath, erected in 1623. It is probably one of the finest tombs that can be found in a parish church anywhere in the country. They are wonderfully sculptured figures, made of plaster and marble. The bodies are painted and the heads and arms are in marble. Our knowledge of costumes over the past centuries has been picked up from tombs like this. Her headdress with the ruff round her neck, the way the folds of her dress lie; his armour and a coronet of metal. Both are painted in the original colours and I gather they have hardly been touched over the centuries. He must have been a patron of the church, for he lies nearest the altar. Such a tomb would have cost something like £500 in those days which, when taking inflation into account, on today's reckoning must have been at least equivalent to £100,000. There are two more tombs to the same family and on the walls are what are called "cartouches" which are shaped tomb stones, which display the name of the deceased and something of

their history. The fine upright effigy is of the fifth Countess of Bath. She had cartouches for all her relations, but she ran out of money so if you look closely at some of the cartouches in the South Chancel aisle you will find they are wood painted to look like marble.

Tawstock Church has another rarity. It is a squire's pew. The Earls of Bath used it, for it kept out the draught during the sermons which went on and on for ages. The Earl had a sightline where he could see the sermon timer on the pulpit. There were one or two luxuries to be had. A comfortable seat to start with, and whilst those sermons dragged on he built up a bit of a thirst so he tapped on a small side panel and a servant passed him through what I can only call a swift half! Certain authorities say that they drank so much, the service taking so long, that they had space for a little chamber pot underneath. Now I am not sure about that but as the Georgians were pretty basic, I wouldn't be the least surprised!

St Just-in-Penwith Methodist Church
CORNWALL

St Just-In-Penwith, way down in the far end of Cornwall, boasts a splendid Georgian Methodist Church.

I am always talking about the interior of our mediaeval churches being blazoned with colour but here in one of the largest Methodist Churches in the West Country, you can see how the lovely subtle colours on the walls and ceilings blend beautifully together with the pale greens, creams, light blues and reds of the glazed window.

It is the farthest west example of Georgian architecture. Built in 1832 and consecrated in 1833, it was almost built in Victorian times for the simple reason that craftsmanship as we know it filtered slowly to the extreme regions of the country. What was "high fashion" in London took twenty or thirty years to filter into Cornwall.

The Georgian plaster motifs are exquisite, particularly the ceiling roses, great circular shapes richly coloured in strong yellows, reds and blues.

The mahogany pulpit is finely detailed. Roman Ionic columns support the entablature,

on top of which is the pulpit. The base is built of stone supported underneath by a spandrel arch. Above it is the great organ which must have thundered out so many times to the huge congregations, numbering some twelve hundred or more, who worshipped here during the nineteenth and early twentieth centuries.

You do not often find memorial tablets in Methodist Churches but there is one here which is quite intriguing it reads: "Erected by public subscription to the memory of 20 miners, some of who were members of this church and congregation, who were drowned by the inrush of water at West Wheel Owles Mine, January 10th 1893."

A poignant memorial indeed. The Reverend Howard Curnow told me what had actually happened.

Apparently the miners broke through by accident, into another chamber mine which earlier had been abandoned and flooded, and the twenty miners were drowned.

Most of the major deaths that occurred at the time were trapped miners but sad as this was, an even greater sadness was the staggering amount of children who died in early infancy, mostly due to childhood illnesses, which we have controlled today. Howard has burial records, page after page, listing sons and daughters, many unnamed, who are just a few months old. Gravestones outside are a poignant reminder to us all.

St Enodoc Church, Trebetherick

CORNWALL

One of the loveliest settings for a Parish Church is St Enodoc at Trebetherick in North Cornwall. John Betjeman had a summer home here and admits to a great affection for the church, delightfully situated, as it is in the middle of a golf course. In his book, "Church Poems," he sets the scene in a poem entitled:
"Sunday Afternoon Service in St Enodoc Church Cornwall"

> *"Come on! Come on! This hillock hides the spire,*
> *Now that one and now none. As winds about*
> *The burnished path through lady's finger, thyme*
> *And bright varieties of saxifrage,*
> *So grows the tinny tenor, faint or loud*
> *And all things draw towards St Enodoc.*
> *Come on! come on! and it is five to three.*
> *Paths, unfamiliar to golfer's brogues,*
> *Cross the eleventh fairway broadside on*
> *And leave the fourteenth tee for thirteenth green,*
> *Ignoring Royal and Ancient, bound for God."*

Sir John Betjeman, my great hero, lies buried in St Enodoc churchyard. He has a tombstone, of Cornish slate, and carved on it the simplest of Epitaphs, in highly ornate lettering: "John Betjeman 1906 to 1984".

I had hoped to attend the funeral but was unable to come and pay my respects until a week later. It was a plain earthen-covered grave with several bunches of wilting flowers and right in the middle of them was a little plastic cup of thunder daisies. I took a photograph because I felt sure that he, above all, would have appreciated that simple token of affection more than all the great bunches of roses and wreaths. For he not only loved Cornwall but he loved the Cornish people as well.

Just across the churchyard is his mother's grave, so he was close to her, and inside the church is a memorial plaque to his father.

He loved this church; he called it "Sinking Neddy" but why such an unusual name? For centuries the sand dunes had come and gone, moved by tide and wind and the little church had disappeared. It was not until the beginning of the eighteenth century, when a man was walking his dog, for they walked their dogs then just as we do today, that he found a triangular, pointed stone about three feet high sticking up out of the ground. He had never noticed it before but obviously a strong wind had swept away the sand, revealing what proved to be the tip of the spire! The villagers came and dug

around and down, eventually finding the church roof intact. They opened up the roof, dropped through onto the floor and found the interior intact. The first service was held on that very day and services have been regularly held here ever since.

Sir John's poem continues by describing the inside of this charming church far better than any words of mine could ever do:

"Then the cool silence of St Enodoc.
My eyes, recovering in the sudden shade,
Discern the long-known little things within –
A map of France in damp above my pew,
Grey-blue of granite in the small arcade
(Late Perp; and not a Parker specimen
But roughly hewn on windy Bodmin Moor),
The modest windows palely glazed with green,
The smooth slate floor, the rounded wooden roof,
The Norman arch, the cable-moulded font –
All have a humble and West Country look."

⁓ *Five* ⁓
HERITAGE

Our landscape is often enhanced by buildings which are designed for specific purposes – buildings like Law Courts or Council Chambers – places in which history just can not help being made. The Old Court House at Dorchester, where the Tolpuddle martyrs were tried and sentenced, readily springs to mind as does Exeter's Guildhall; the oldest Council Chamber in Britain where the City Council still meets. It owes its present appearance just as much to the building stone used as it does to its intricately carved exterior. The stone used came from nearby Beer quarry, one of a handful in the country, which dates back to Roman times and is open for the public to visit.

Beer Quarries in the olden days

Beer Quarry Caves
EAST DEVON

The small seaside village of Beer in East Devon can really boast of a fascinating piece of England's heritage, Quarry Caves, which date back to Roman times.

My guide was John Scott a co-tenant with Mrs Gladys Grey. John has a natural enthusiasm for the quarry caves, as his own father actually worked there and John tells a fascinating story as he shows you round.

The most difficult thing for people to imagine when they first go down into the caves is the sheer size of the place. Beneath the hill are seventy-three and a half acres of quarried space. It is not a natural cave but one hewn by men quarrying the stone, by hand, in order to make a living. They quarried the stone that has been used in some of the most famous buildings in the country. Two thousand years ago the hill was solid limestone. The Romans cut out the entrance, through which visitors enter today. They were the first to find Beer stone and discovered that the optimum height they could cut out was a twenty-foot high layer, leaving a ceiling and floor full of fossils. You never find any fossils in the Beer stone itself for it is a beautiful stone, highly suitable for fine detailed carving. They also discovered that when you took the stone outside and into the air it not only dried to a lovely creamy colour but became five

An aerial view of Beer Head

times harder than when first cut out. The Romans had high regard for the stone and not only used it to build their own villas, but they also transported blocks from here over twenty miles to help build Roman Exeter, or "Isca" to give it its Roman name. For me the most fascinating part was seeing the actual axe marks made by the Roman quarrymen – easily discernible in the now electrically lit caves. So two thousand years of "hard graft" at the quarry has made it the size it is today.

To appreciate this most unusual place, it is best to try to imagine what it must have been like to actually work here. It was not just the men but whole families. In those early days Beer village was isolated. Everybody had to work or else the village died so if people were unable to go fishing or farming they were obliged to work the quarry caves.

Only one hundred or so years ago Lucy Harmer was put to work here and she was paid to take oil around to the quarrymen for their lamps, and to feed the horses. Not a bad job but records tell us that she was only eight years old at the time! There were two basic jobs, the quarrymen who cut out the stone and the stone masons. They were the better paid of the two making beautiful carvings for churches in the candlelit caves.

One such piece of carving was the original church window made for the West window of Colyton Church (see chapter on Colyton Church). A replacement stands today in Colyton Church. The original was carved, in the quarry, by seven freemasons from Beer village. They managed to carve the whole window by candlelight, in fifty-eight pieces. The Victorians replaced it in the church, although from what John says, it was perfectly all right at that time.

A few years ago, a master mason, Peter Day of Exeter and John Scott, found the original pieces in the churchyard and rebuilt it in the quarry caves. They even checked on the masons marks in the records and found the names of the men who had carved it five centuries ago.

The Normans worked with pick axes in the main, but later, handsaws were used and the quarrymen always wrote their names on the quarry wall to prove how much stone they had worked each day. Their names, particularly those of John Hayes and George Rossiter, can be read quite easily. They had worked the first hacksaws down here, on an old Norman pillar in 1750. The sentences look as fresh today as they did then, nearly three hundred years ago.

The saying "stone deaf" is a poignant reminder of the grim conditions there. With one hundred men all working with sledge hammers the sound must have reverberated in a horrifying way around the caves and most quarry men were "stone deaf" after only a few years. John demonstrates the awesome sound by banging on a stone with a simple plastic crash helmet, which you are obliged to wear on a visit.

The caves are well worth a visit but do wear a woolly for the temperature is a constant 55 °F (12–13 °C).

We only have to look around at many of our beautiful Cathedrals today and appreciate that the stone from these great caves has been used to build some of our great churches. It makes me feel grateful to the successive generations of Beer quarrymen who have worked these caves for two thousand years thereby enriching our heritage by their efforts.

Guildhall, Exeter

DEVON

The façade of the Guildhall in Exeter is built of Beer stone, taken from the quarry. It is a wonderful, early example of the Renaissance style of architecture. Greek motif columns divide large Tudor windows on the main front. This perfect façade was ornamental when built, for such fronts were painted in glorious bright reds, blues, gold and silver paints. There is no detailed record as to how it would have appeared in its heyday. My sketch shows how I believe it might have looked. It would have sparkled in the sunshine like a jewel box, covered in a myriad of lovely bright colours. Sadly it would not be possible to repaint it today as the stone has eroded over the centuries so much that it would be virtually impossible to apply the colours successfully. What a pity!

Incidentally, many Cathedral fronts were painted in a similar manner. This we know, as fragments of original colour have been found when restoration took place and Exeter Cathedral had a particularly colourful front, similar in colour to the Guildhall.

The Guildhall is considered to be the oldest Council Chamber, still in regular use, for Council meetings. The main entrance is through an immensely strong looking door, dated 1593. It is a Judas Gate, a door within a door, the idea being that you could keep out a whole army with just one swordsman standing there, nor was there room for a horseman to ride through either.

The Guildhall as we see it today, dates from the fifteenth century, 1470 or thereabouts and the great high roof is most impressive. The arch-braced roof of seven bays is unusual in so far as there is an upper coved section, above trusses, rather like church work, and there are bosses at the junctions of the purlins and intermediate trusses. The roof was built by

local Exeter-based carpenters. Much of the wall panelling is contemporary with the roof. The Mayor's chair was made in 1697 and presides over the hanging portraits of previous Mayors and their Coats of Arms. Most of the other furnishings, including the stained glass windows, are Victorian.

As you might expect, the Guildhall has many treasures which have been donated over the centuries. They are on display in the gallery. Even more significant for me, are the regalia used on ceremonial occasions. There are four mace bearers who carry the civic maces, and Chris Lambert, Mace Sergeant at Arms, showed them to me. One, made by John Riggs of London and dated 1730, is silver gilt and has the Royal Coat of Arms in the centre with the Civic Coat of Arms on the side.

The ceremonial sword and cap of Maintenance recalls Henry VII's visit to the city in 1497. The right of the city to bear a sword, with the sword bearer wearing the cap, was given to the city at that time to show his gratitude to the citizens of Exeter, who had resisted the rebel army of Perkin Warbeck, a pretender to the throne. A marvellous treasure, but there is yet another group of even older treasured items.

The wait's chains – there are four of them – are fine delicate chains, originally worn by the waits, the musicians or town band who played for the Mayoral banquets, Coronations, Victories and at Christmas. The four waits paraded with the Mayor around the city with their little flutes and drums on such "high days and holidays". These exquisite chains are now believed to date back to 1330. Unique and precious today, all four, made of solid silver cost just four shillings (20p) when they were made!

What a wonderful heritage for any city to have. Such

EXETER. — The Guildhall.

items belong as much to the past as to the future generations. We are today merely their custodians.

Courthouse, Dorchester and Tolpuddle
DORSET

Law Courts and Council Chambers are places in which history is made, where democracy and the freedom of the individual are all important, but at the old Crown Court at Dorchester only one hundred and fifty years ago, things were not as they should have been. Here the six Tolpuddle Martyrs were found guilty of treason and sentenced by the judge to be transported to Australia for seven years; a truly harsh sentence.

It all started in the small Dorset village of Tolpuddle where early trade unionism reached its peak and the movement found its first martyrs, six local men. Farm labourer's wages in the 1830s were then about eight shillings a week, and employers were reducing them to six shillings, taking the wage well below the poverty line. Negotiations proved useless and on the advice of the Grand National Consolidated Trades Union the men formed a Friendly Society of Agricultural Labourers. Now this in itself did not break the law, but by taking an oath of unity, they fell foul of the Mutiny Act of 1797 and were duly arrested. There is little doubt that this was an excuse by the authorities to make examples of them and to deter others from arranging themselves into trade unions.

The six farm workers were sentenced to seven years transportation, such an exceptionally harsh sentence that it brought howls of protest from the crowds in the Dorchester Courtroom at the time, for the charges brought against them were entirely unfounded.

The actual words used by the judge pronouncing sentence were as follows:

"The object of all legal punishment is not altogether with a view of operating on the defenders themselves, it is also for the sake of offering the example and warning and accordingly the offence of which you have been convicted after evidence was perfectly satisfactory. The crime to a conviction of which that evidence has led is of that description that the security of the country and the maintenance of the laws on the upholding of those the welfare of this country depends, make it necessary for me to pass on you the sentence required by those laws. I feel that I have no discretion in the matter but I am bound to pronounce on you the sentence which the act of parliament has imposed. And I therefore adjudge you and each of you, George Loveless, James Loveless, James Hammett, Thomas Standfield, John Standfield and James Brine shall be transported to such places beyond the seas that his Majesty's Council in their discretion shall see fit – for the term of seven years."

The twelve jury men at the trial, mostly farmers themselves, took only five minutes to come to a decision. The six men were brought from the courtroom and incarcerated in dreadful cells, directly below the courtroom. Grim and dark they were however not so forbidding, as was the adjacent pit where w o m e n prisoners were held. The only ventilation and light were through a row of holes drilled into the woodwork, below the judge's seat, in the court above. The six men were sent to Australia, a nightmare journey which took several months. Once there, they were sold as "slaves", for £1 each, to whoever would buy them. Five of them worked in a penal colony, chained together for two years. One of them, James Hammett, was sent to a sheep farm in Tasmania but was still treated as a "slave".

Back home there was a terrific uproar in the country as a result of the dreadful decision. Some 800,000 people petitioned the then Home Secretary who passed it to the House of Commons. Eventually they won their reprieve and were given their freedom and a Royal Pardon. There being no other communication, other than by mail aboard ship, it took many months for the pardons to reach the men and it was not until eighteen months later that five of them returned to Plymouth, to a heroes' welcome. The sixth man, James Hammett, still working on the sheep farm, happened to pick up an old newspaper, four years later and read of the pardon. He was the only one of the six to return to the village, where he became a builder. His grave is in the churchyard. The other five had been given farms in Essex but all of them having married, decided to emigrate to Canada where they lived out their lives, as much respected citizens. John Standfield became Mayor of his district.

In 1934 the TUC built six cottages as a tribute to the six martyrs, each one bearing the name of a martyr. In the middle of these is now a Museum commemorating the "Tolpuddle Martyrs". The Georgian Courtroom, at Dorchester, with its columns holding up the

galleries on either side, was still in use up to 1955, when a new Crown Court was opened up in the County Council Offices. The Arms of George III, hang above the judge's seat. The paint work is cream and brown, popular colours for public buildings at the time, whilst the walls are pale green. The Georgian windows are probably the first example of double glazing – two identical windows, on interior and exterior walls with a substantial gap between them.

Wynard's Almshouses, Exeter
DEVON

The cobbled courtyard at Wynard's Almshouses, in the centre of Exeter, is a wonderful, peaceful oasis tucked away from the noise of the city traffic close by. Originally, before becoming Almshouses, it was a leper hospital, which was completely self-contained within the court yard. It still has its own little well. Drainage however was always a problem in those days, they often used to throw accumulated rubbish out of the upper windows!

The patients all had little individual units of their own, built in gentle red sandstone, a local Devon red stone, which is warm to look at. But as can be seen, it weathers very easily, so much so that it has actually recessed back from the harder lighter coloured stone which forms the quoins to the chimney and window surrounds.

The chimneys are at least twelve feet tall, reaching above the ridge of the roof. They have to be that high for the flue to draw properly otherwise there are problems of pressure in such a small area. They are built of red brick, matching brick for the quoins as well – this gives a clue to the fact that the Almshouses had been restored at sometime and sure enough they were in about the 1850s. The little window over the centre cottage has the heads of patron William Wynyard and his wife sculptured into the window surround.

Today this lovely courtyard has another use altogether. No longer is it an almshouse or a hospital. It is still catering for Exeter's needs. The small houses accommodate the Samaritans, The Citizen's Advice Bureau, and Relate. Even the little chapel is used, just as it was originally. How marvellous it is to see an historic building like this still serving the community in such a comforting way.

St John Almshouses, Sherborne
DORSET

In the unique, unspoilt town of Sherborne in Dorset and in the shadow of the magnificent Abbey, stands the fifteenth century almshouses. As was the custom in

those days, with such buildings, they were built to look imposing because in most cases the benefactors who paid for them to be built wished it so. The almshouses have hardly changed at all in five hundred years and are still very much in use today, still administered by twelve Brethren (local businessmen) as they have been over the centuries. Part of the almshouses are open to the public and Joan Gillard, one of the guides at St John Almshouses told me how the house had been founded in 1437. She told me that a Royal Licence was granted by Henry VI because almshouses had to have a Royal Licence before they could be built. Joan is proud to feel that they have the actual

document bearing the date 11th July 1437 and it carries the Royal Seal dated 1437. It is Latin and is considered to be a rare and precious document.

The chapel is atmospheric, it seems to emanate from the unique triptych. It is a German copy of a Flemish painting from about 1480 and it is

contemporary with the house. The two side panels fold across the larger centre panel which depicts the raising of Lazarus. It is a glorious picture of national importance. The large oak screen similar to a rood screen is unusual also in so far as it has doors in the screen which are made from one complete piece of oak. Each door has been cut from a single piece with not a joint in it. It is very unusual to see doors made this way.

Above the screen is a gallery, for sick or bedridden inmates. For in earlier times one of the rules was that residents should attend chapel services six or seven times a day. One wonders how they found time to do anything else for such services might well each have lasted at least an hour!

The women originally lived in one part of the house separated from the men. Those who lived on the first floor had to negotiate a stone, outside staircase. That original staircase is still here although it is now encased in wood and internal.

The original costumes worn by the inmates are still on display – red cloaks for the women with a black bonnet and rather magnificent black Melton cloth coats for the men, with the emblem of the house, the Bishop's Mitre. This badge commemorates Bishop Neville of Salisbury who interceded with the King for the granting of the original licence. The emblem is also on the pewter ware. Every piece is stamped with it. The pewter plates are displayed and were still used until the First World War. The dresser on which they are displayed was made specially by a local joiner in 1914, and cost £19. It is a magnificent piece of furniture and was made at a very reasonable price even by today's standards.

In the lovely grass and cobbled courtyard, surrounded on all sides by flowers I met the present matron, Mary Woods. Her post was originally known as "House-wife." Everything is still run much as it always was. Except that she now has eighteen residents instead of the original twelve. Mary is pleased to see a perfect balance with nine women and nine men.

There used to be two separate dormitories one for men and one for women but now each has his or her own little bedsit, with a handbasin and television and so really they can be free to be alone or to enjoy the company of the others in the sitting room or dining room. No longer are they required to attend chapel six or seven times a day but just once during the week.

Of course the marvellous thing is that they are right in the centre of this lovely town and can wander out for walks and shopping. Years ago the doors were locked at 6 o'clock at night whereas today all the residents have a key of their own.

It really is a charming, delightful and friendly house. I think I will book my place right away!

Sidholme, Sidmouth
DEVON

The delightful nineteenth century Regency resort of Sidmouth, with its elegant esplanade, abounds in architectural gems, some tucked away in hidden corners such as the glorious building known as "Sidholme", in the delightfully named "Elysian Fields".

The house was once the home of the Duke and Duchess of Buckingham. He had sold his London home, Buckingham House, to George III, who turned it into Buckingham Palace, home of Monarchs ever since. Having settled in the Duchess fell out with the local vicar and she insisted on designing a chapel for herself to be built onto the house. The room, designed as a chapel, was never used as such for she made her peace with the vicar and the huge extension was eventually transformed into a quite wonderful music room.

The house is now an hotel run by the Methodist Holiday Guild and the music room is still used as such. It is a stunning room, designed in the Baroque style of architecture with all the best features of a chapel. Artists from Italy were especially commissioned to do the art work, craftsmen who came over and spent their life working on these sort of architectural features. They decorated the soaring columns on either side of the windows – lovely pillars with tiny balls at the top forming intricate patterned capitals, painted cherubs, playing and singing away, contained within four triangular paintings on the ceiling of the great domed and vaulted roof. There is a fine fireplace in marble with a Baroque mirror above and the walls are covered in superb wallpaper topped by highly decorative wall paintings. There is still a hint of a chapel, for the splendid organ is still here. The greatest joy for me, of all features in the room, are the wonderful chandeliers.

For the television programme, we stepped back in time, staging a musical soirée, much as it would have been at the turn of the century. Artists, baritone William Parish and pianist Betty Parr, performing one of Ralph Vaughn William's "Songs of Travel" to an elegantly dressed, appreciative audience, made up of members of the Sidmouth Arts Club Operatic Society, evoking the ambience of a more genteel age, so very appropriate to this lovely music room.

···━━◉━━···

❧ *Six* ❧
MINIATURES

T he toys we play with as children are, so often, miniature versions of things we encounter later as adults– from train sets to cars, farm animals to dolls houses. These scaled down versions are fascinating, for we are all children at heart.

The West Country, for some reason, seems to have more than its fair share of scaled down models of each and every sort, model villages, models of the world, famous monuments, scale models of historic houses, castles, gypsy caravans and even miniature gardens and miniature flowers. But what is even more surprising is that the region is rich with talented folk whose lives are spent making and caring for all of these things.

So let's set off on a journey which was not so much "Gulliver's Travels" as "G'Oliver's Travels"!

Babbacombe Model Village
DEVON

As an architect I am particularly intrigued by model buildings, especially those at Babbacombe in South Devon; one of the finest model villages in the world. Indeed it was the first in the world and there are several copies in other countries. It has just about everything, and is actually built in the same way as real dwellings and public buildings and they are completely weather proof.

Owner and former estate agent, Tom Dobbins came here during the winter of 1963.

He had designed a model village at Southport, but the area available was just not big enough, so he and his wife came to Babbacombe and built this delightful model village. It covers five acres and has already taken Tom and his talented team over thirty years to build. But to call it a village is hardly fair any more, as there is everything here from a football stadium to a power station. His aim is to copy life as much as possible, if he passes along a street and sees a window cleaner, then a window cleaner is popped into the village. Seeing a fire engine, he thought he'd have a house on fire, and sure enough there it is, a thatched cottage blazing away, complete

In the land of giants?

A nudist beach ... in the model village

with fire engines and firemen in attendance! Important to the enjoyment are the sound effects, music, and Tom's sense of humour. Visitors love the authenticity of the sound effects – such as the toilets flushing, as you pass the miniature toilet block!

All the models are made on site in the workshops. Upkeep is important, because the buildings can be affected by extremes of weather. Dedicated staff carry out constant repairs, much in the same way as we do our own houses. There are thirty thousand tiny people "living" in the village, and even they are continually being repainted, replaced, changed and updated.

Tom Dobbins admits that his favourite is always the "next" model. The latest miniature is a perfect "Stonehenge". Tom gets inspiration from visitors who offer many ideas and suggestions. I could not resist mentioning a television crew? Sure enough, Tom pointed out a perfect replica crew with cameras, lights, OB van, the lot. Even a presenter and his dog!

There are at least fifteen copies of this village in other countries, ranging from New Zealand, to Thailand and most of the owners have sought Tom's advice; he is proud to have been their inspiration.

The most magic moments for me are after dark when the whole five acres are suddenly plunged into darkness, and two "space craft" in the shape of flying saucers appear, floating in the sky, with laser beams and flashing lights. They are an awesome, highly realistic sight; yet another of Tom's inspired ideas. If you are anywhere near Babbacombe, do go and visit this fantastic model village and do hang on until darkness comes. It is well worth it.

Goonhavern World Models
CORNWALL

The most marvellous collection of model buildings of the world is at Goonhavern, near Newquay in Cornwall.

Jules Verne's "Around the World in Eighty Days" has nothing on this. At Goonhavern you need only a few hours to complete an equally incredible "journey" seeing most of all the great buildings of the world.

Where better to start our "World Tour" in miniature, than the cradle of civilisation in the land surrounding the Mediterranean sea. The Great Sphinx and the Pyramids of Egypt are as impressive as the originals. Greece is represented by a wonderful restoration of the Parthenon, showing how the temple would have looked, before it became the famous ruin we know today.

The scale of the leaning Tower of Pisa is perfect. The original was a hundred and seventy feet high and as it was being built there was apparently insufficient strength in the subsoil or the foundations and the tower started to lean, even before the building was finished. A little bell turret was put on top in the hope that it would act as a counterbalance, which cants the other way. This made little difference. It has stood like that since the fifteenth century, but has been moving at the rate of about a centimetre a year and is now 4.28 metres (14 feet) out of true. Many experiments have been carried out over the centuries, the current one of pumping many tons of lead into the foundations appears to be successful. I certainly hope that this time it will stabilise, because it is such a lovely and unusual monument.

In Goonhavern's "India" is the Taj Mahal, an ornate marble mausoleum built by a Prince for his favourite wife. In the mystic East we have the Kyota Temple in Japan, the original, now a zen temple, was built in 1397. On to the Easter Islands in the Pacific where we find our first statues, magnificent legless figures, whose origin is still a mystery today. These chaps are not just legless but body-less as well.

On a superb model of the Mount Rushmore heads, carved in the

Black Hills of South Dakota, we can see the enormous heads of four American

presidents. These faces are one hundred feet high and carved from granite whereas the replica models at Goonhavern are all made in fine detail of fibreglass and concrete.

New York's Statue of Liberty is said to have been modelled by Isabella, wife of Isaac Singer of sewing machine fame.

On our visit, the White House of America received an unscheduled visitor. "Oliver" walked across the "lawns" giving us a superb example of the "scale" of the models. It is also interesting to be able to walk around the back of the White House, a view we are not able to see so often. I personally think it is more attractive than the front.

Back on this side of the Atlantic, Paris is represented, of course, by Eiffel's masterpiece tower. Europe's highest structure, it is just short of being a thousand feet high.

The Swiss Chalet is a fine example of the modeller's art – the same wood has been used as in the original. Another timber building is the Stave church in Norway, so called because the walls are tree trunks split vertically in two.

Finally to Britain, where better than an easily recognisable Stonehenge, as it was in all its glory, two thousand or more years ago. They were not "changing guard" at Buckingham Palace in 1762 for it was then the home of the Duke of Buckingham, who sold it to George III and it has been the London home of the sovereign ever since. This superb replica is gazed upon by Britannia who, quite rightly, dominates this fascinating "World in Miniature".

Gypsy Caravans
CORNWALL

Near Liskeard in Cornwall, I found talented husband and wife team, Lance and June Stapely creating, with a rare skill, the most exquisite miniature Gypsy caravans. Lance started making models about forty years ago when he took a keen interest in a gypsy family who regularly spent a few weeks at his father's smallholding. He was fascinated

Photo: Evening Herald, Plymouth

by their way of living but even more by their caravans. There and then he set about making his first model. The models are built to scale, usually to one twelfth, using wood, lime, beech or tulip wood, birch and metal, for he makes everything, each and every part, all immaculately detailed and hand carved,

Each wagon takes up to three hundred hours to assemble, ready for painting. The miniature details are perfect. There are lamps that light up, a spindle rack for spare harnesses, a hen box where bantams would be housed, even a tiny bucket for slops.

The wheels too are made in the same manner as are real ones; built in segments, the spokes are shaped and set up on a jig. Lance has his own trademark, which is an aluminium bracket and he also signs his name underneath each caravan.

The painting, finishing and furnishing is done beautifully by June Stapely. She uses the authentic colours, maroon, red, and dark green, the colours favoured by the gypsy folk. The use of gold leaf signifies the gypsy hierarchy. The richer they were, the more gold leaf they displayed; using even more each time the caravan was redecorated. They are magnificent and June spends a hundred or so hours on each one. She also makes the curtains, bedding, etched and engraved mirrors and even paints the tiny willow pattern plates. The furniture is highly varnished. It is a delight to see such intricate and quite charming works of art still being made exclusively in the West Country and selling all over the world.

Not open to the public

Olde Romany Plant Remedies

Blackberry

Olde Romany Plant Remedies

Travellers Joy

House That Moved, Exeter
DEVON

The oldest, continuously inhabited house in the West Country stands opposite the church of St Mary Steps in Exeter, a delightful half-timbered dwelling. However it did not start life there. Originally built in the old city centre, the house survived the blitz of the Second World War, when much of the centre of Exeter was damaged by bombs, only to find itself under fire of a different sort when it stood in the way of a redevelopment scheme in 1964. The six hundred-year-old building was considered to be of sufficient historical value to save and this was achieved by removing it three hundred yards on a trackway and rollers up the road to its new home.

At Barnstaple in North Devon brothers Alan and Gerry Welch specialise in making scale models of half-timbered Tudor buildings. The models are exquisite and they have made a one twelfth scale model "House that Moved" which is perfect in every detail. It has been constructed in exactly the same way as the original house, six hundred years ago. Alan uses hard wood which is stained to match the original and each piece of timber is carved by hand. There are leaded windows, a tiled roof, even real paving stones. The frame, a timber skeleton has infilled panels. Each storey juts out, or overhangs, the one below with the smallest at the bottom. This limited floor area saved rates in the old days, because premises were rated on the ground floor space. The over hanging of the upper storeys was a sneaky way of extending the floor space.

The real thing

The structure inside is equally accurate, down to the last detail. The beams are as the originals with a Dragon Beam (that is a diagonal tie beam) used on buildings with two jeted sides, tying the structure together. It must have been as delicate a job to get the balance just right in the model, as it was in the original building.

Gerry showed me how the leaded windows were made using liquid lead and glass. The system, just like the originals, was a time-consuming job. They also make stained glass windows using this method.

The tiny models of furniture and ornaments in the house, which are all to scale, are made by craftsmen, all of whom live and work in the West Country. From a minute toolkit, immaculate in detail, made by Terry McAllister, to a wooden cabinet made by Brian Masters of Cullompton. The house, furnished throughout contained so many fascinating things, a tiny pair of pliers that really work, pewter ware, china, and a ticking, chiming "antique" wall clock. It never fails to amaze me how many talented artists and craftsmen we have here in the West Country

Not surprisingly, these lovely Tudor houses are made to order, and sell all over the world. "The House that Moved" featured here, has been made for an American for £1,000, the average cost of such a model, unfurnished of course (the furniture would cost about another £1,000). How marvellous to think of such a fine examples of West Country heritage, and craftsmanship being exported. Brothers, Alan and Gerry Welch are certainly waving the flag not only for England but also for North Devon as well.

Bonsai Trees, Honiton
DEVON

I have always loved Bonsai trees and when I paid a visit to the Bonsai Trees and Miniature Gardens Nursery, near Honiton, owner Irene Thresher explained to me that the word Bonsai actually means "tree in a pot", so any kind of tree, shrub or plant can be used. The tree stays in the pot and these perfect miniatures can last for hundreds of years.

Irene and her husband Don take great delight in their work and the miniature gardens, so beautifully laid out, are a joy to wander around. Here you will find little tableaux with tiny houses, set in their own gardens, a whole range of miniature plants, even the tiniest rose in the world. A fully grown miniature rose bush (about two inches tall) only costs about £2.

There is a seaside scene with Lichen, Lipwort, Starweed and all the natural things which make up a beach scene. There is a small Spirea and a lot of the ground cover plant is on display. Praetia with its little blue flower, the tiny Chrysanthemum flowers look wonderful in the sunshine. The Rhoda Hypocsis, which Irene assures me is very easy to grow, comes in all different shades and flowers all summer long.

Don makes all the tiny buildings to a 1:32 scale, and they are exquisite, built of natural materials to withstand the outdoor life.

They were recently invited to exhibit at the Chelsea Flower Show where their unique stand was much appreciated and proved to be a great crowd puller.

Their greatest achievement, to date, is that they are the only nursery in the world to have actually exported Bonsai to the Japanese! How about that? One for the record books for sure!

Corfe Model Village
DORSET

I have already written of the scale model Corfe Castle in the "Castles" chapter but the castle is only part of a complete model of Corfe village. I could not resist revisiting to describe the delightful model village which is tucked away in the back garden of one of the many attractive houses in Corfe's main street. All the model houses are built of natural stone with tiled and slated roofs. What I found most fascinating of all is that there is a model of the actual house and garden, and

in that garden is a model of the house and garden! And in that garden is an even tinier model of the house and garden. And so on! An inspired model well worth the visit to Corfe in miniature.

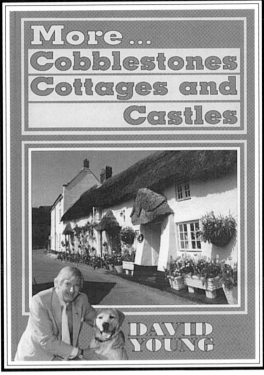

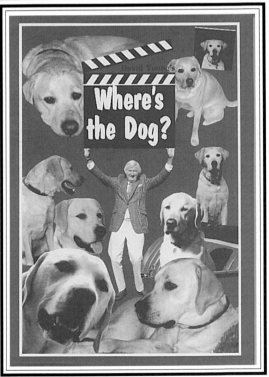

David Young has written several books to accompany and complement his television career. Available from the address below, these include: *Cobblestones, Cottages and Castles* (£12.95); *More ...Cobblestones, Cottages and Castles* (£9.95); *An A to Z of Villages* (£4.95) and *Where's the Dog?* (£9.95) which delightfully tells the amazing and amusing incidents that have happened to him and his companions in over three decades of local television filming.

Obelisk Publications
2 Church Hill
Pinhoe
Exeter, Devon
EX4 9ER   Tel: Exeter 468556